BEATLES LEGENDS ALPHABET

Words by Robin Feiner

Aa

A is for **A** Day In The Life. I read the news today, oh boy. The jewel in the crown of the acclaimed Sgt. Pepper's album. Playing big ideas – like death and war – against our daily grind, this radical masterpiece builds to a cacophony of noise that loves to turn you on.

Bb

B is for Blackbird.
This delicate lullaby of a
song plucks and harmonizes
its way from the light of the
dark black night and into our
hearts. Featuring on The White
Album, Blackbird is an ode to
the struggle fought by African
American women during the
civil rights movement –
waiting for this moment
to arise.

C is for Come Together. Grooving up slowly, with joo joo eyeballs and hair down to his knee, Come Together is full of good vibrations and out-there imagery. Written as a call to arms for the hippy movement, it's both smooth and gritty, like a roller coaster and muddy water coming together, right now, over me.

D is for **D**ay Tripper.
A huge hit for the band
with its driving beat, twanging
guitar and swinging groove,
Day Tripper is a lively, playful
pop song aimed at the hearts
of teenage girls. Like a one-
way ticket or a Sunday drive,
it's a big teaser that leaves
you wanting more.

E is for Eleanor Rigby. With its beautiful string arrangement, this sad tale of loneliness tugs at the heart. Eleanor Rigby waits at the window and lives in a dream as Father McKenzie writes a sermon that no one will hear, until one day, when their paths cross. All the lonely people, where do they all belong?

F is for Strawberry Fields Forever. Warped, looped and layered, this legendary song challenged traditional Beatles listeners with its wild and psychedelic dreamscape. Like a basket full of deliciousness for your ears, go down to Strawberry Fields Forever where nothing is real, and there's nothing to get hung about.

G is for Get Back. Oozing cool, this is a rambling blues tune about a loner named Jojo who hits the road for California, and Sweet Loretta Martin who's living her best life. With its driving beat and sense of freedom, it's best listened to cruising the freeway with the windows down and the speakers turned up!

H is for **H**ere Comes The Sun. Written and sung by George Harrison and led by the sweetness of his guitar, this joyous ray of light bundles you up and makes you feel warm and fuzzy, like the first day of Spring. Starting delicately and building into a pure pop masterpiece, this song returns smiles to the faces, little darling.

I is for **I** Am The Walrus.
I am the egg man! I am the walrus! Goo goo g'joob! Silly and intentionally confusing, this song is a fantastical journey into the wild imagination of the legendary John Lennon. Its vivid imagery was inspired, in part, by Lewis Carroll's poem, 'The Walrus and the Carpenter'.

J is for Hey Jude.
This legendary singalong
was written by Paul McCartney
for a young Julian Lennon
as his father began a new
relationship with Yoko Ono.
It's an uplifting song about
seeing the good in hard
situations. When you let love
in, you can begin to make
things better, better, Better,
BETTER!

K is for Sun **K**ing. Everybody's laughing and everybody's happy in this dreamy little jingle that floats onto Abbey Road like a sun beam, warm-hearted and weightless. Adding to the summery vibe is a mix of Italian, Spanish and Portuguese lyrics washing over you like the backdrop of a beach holiday. Mi amore!

L is for **Lucy In The Sky With Diamonds.** Playful, visual and cheekily experimental, this is one of the band's most legendary hits. On this curious trip in a boat on a river, with tangerine trees and marmalade skies, your tour guide is a girl with kaleidoscope eyes ... and you're gone.

M is for **Magical Mystery Tour.** Roll up, roll up! This upbeat, energetic track is a fanfare of an adventure. Part rock and roll tour, part traveling circus, the **Magical Mystery Tour** is both a song and a film that's just waiting to take you away.

N is for **N**owhere Man. The man in the song can be anyone really, but it was actually written by John Lennon about himself during a bad case of writer's block. What starts in melancholy soon becomes hopeful. A reassuring reminder that even great people have bad days, and even the worst days can be overcome.

O is for **O**ctopus's Garden. Written and sung by Ringo, this jolly little sea shanty won the heart of fellow Beatle George. Escaping the pressures of daily life in favor of fun and freedom under the ocean, we're invited to a little hideaway beneath the waves, in an octopus's garden, in the shade.

City of Liverpool
PENNY
LANE L18

P is for **P**enny Lane. Strolling down old Penny Lane, The Beatles pay tribute to their childhood neighborhood in Liverpool, England, a place still in their ears and eyes. A place where people stop and say hello. A banker with a motorcar, a fireman with an hourglass. There beneath the blue suburban skies.

Q is for **Q**ueen Elizabeth – Her Majesty. At just 23 seconds, this tongue-in-cheek tribute to Her Majesty Queen Elizabeth II is The Beatles' shortest song. In this silly little ditty, Paul McCartney muses how he'd like to meet her ... an event that happened years later when Her Majesty knighted him!

R is for Lovely **R**ita.
From royalty to meter maids,
The Beatles honor girls from
all walks of life. This lively tune
about a parking warden will
tow your heart away with its
jug-band bass and rag-time
piano playfulness. Lovely Rita,
meter maid, where would
I be without you!

Ss

is for gt. Pepper's Lonely Hearts Club Band. Guaranteed to raise a smile, this song opens the legendary album of the same name. Certainly a thrill, it mixes rock and roll, marching band brass and theatrics to set the scene for 1967's so-called Summer of Love. We hope you will enjoy the show.

T is for Ticket To Ride. Inspired in equal parts by garage rock and Indian raga music, this song cuts a deep, heavy groove that's almost hypnotizing! It tells the story of a girl who leaves her boyfriend and doesn't look back. She's got a ticket to ride, and she don't care!

U is for Back In The U.S.S.R. With its legendary Chuck Berry riffs and sweet Beach Boy harmonies, this spikey rock and roller pays tribute to Mother Russia while tipping a hat to great American music. You don't know how lucky you are, boy! Back in the U.S.S.R!

V is for Love Me Do.
This simple tune that
promises to always be true
is instantly recognizable by
Lennon's sweet harmonica
front and center. As the band's
debut single, it's the song
that would begin the world's
obsession with The Beatles,
offering us someone to
love, somebody new.
P.S. I love you.

Ww

W is for **W**hile My Guitar Gently Weeps. George Harrison's first great composition and one of the band's greatest rock songs, this sprawling and heavy track is about humankind's potential for unconditional love. The love there that's sleeping. It's a theme that still rings true decades later.

X is for Taxman.
Protesting against the government of the day, this loose and groovy tune pokes fun at the thieving tax man. If you drive a car, I'll tax the street. If you try to sit, I'll tax your seat. This cheeky hip-shaker is guaranteed to shimmy the shillings from your shorts!

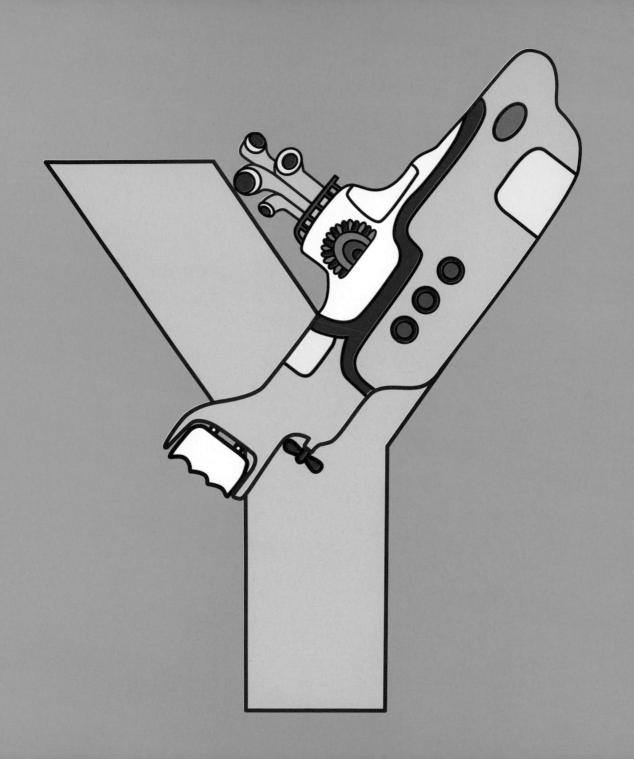

Y is for Yellow Submarine. Written as a children's song, Ringo sings another colorful, playful tune, with the sounds of a calming shoreline lapping your ears. Sky of blue and sea of green, in our Yellow Submarine – it's one of The Beatles' most famous and fun singalongs.

Z is for Dizzy Miss Lizzy. This classic rhythm and blues song originally written and recorded by American Larry Williams is one of many covers made famous by The Beatles. Over twanging guitar, John Lennon cuts loose with woops and yeahs, as he loses his mind over Dizzy Miss Lizzy. Ow!

The ever-expanding legendary library

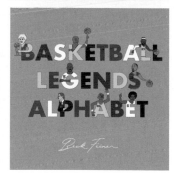

EXPLORE THESE LEGENDARY ALPHABETS & MORE AT WWW.ALPHABETLEGENDS.COM

BEATLES LEGENDS ALPHABET

www.alphabetlegends.com

Published by Alphabet Legends Pty Ltd in 2021
Created by Beck Feiner
Copyright © Alphabet Legends Pty Ltd 2021

Printed and bound in China.

9780648962878

ALPHABET LEGENDS